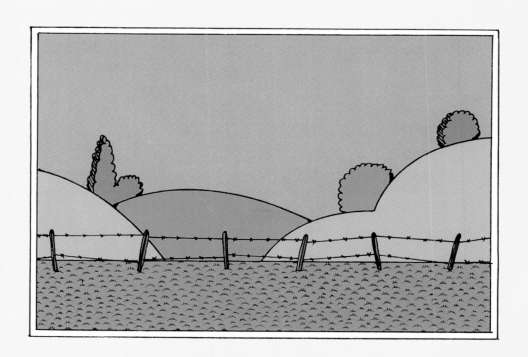

THE MILK MAKERS

By Gail Gibbons

Aladdin Paperbacks

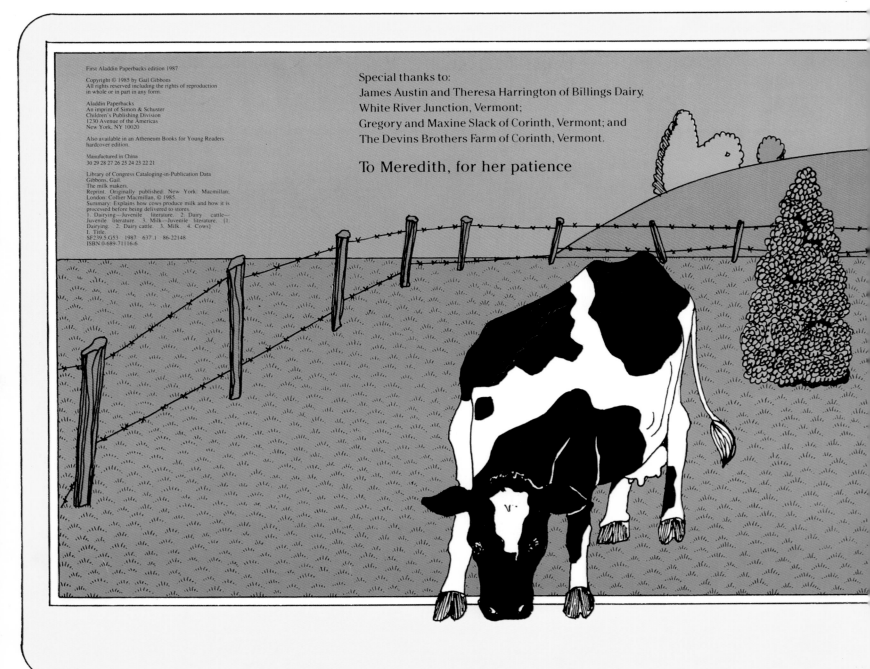

First Aladdin Paperbacks edition 1987

Aladdin Paperbacks
An imprint of Simon & Schuster
Children's Publishing Division
1230 Avenue of the Americas
New York, NY 10020

Also available in an Atheneum Books for Young Readers
hardcover edition.

Manufactured in China
30 29 28 27 26 25 24 23 22 21

Library of Congress Cataloging-in-Publication Data
Gibbons, Gail.
The milk makers.
Reprint. Originally published: New York: Macmillan;
London: Collier Macmillan, © 1985.
Summary: Explains how cows produce milk and how it is
processed before being delivered to stores.
1. Dairying—Juvenile literature. 2. Dairy cattle—
Juvenile literature. 3. Milk—Juvenile literature. [1.
Dairying. 2. Dairy cattle. 3. Milk. 4. Cows]
I. Title.
SF239.5.G53 1987 637.1 86-22148
ISBN 0-689-71116-6

Special thanks to:
James Austin and Theresa Harrington of Billings Dairy,
White River Junction, Vermont;
Gregory and Maxine Slack of Corinth, Vermont; and
The Devins Brothers Farm of Corinth, Vermont.

To Meredith, for her patience

Cows are grazing in an open meadow. They are dairy cows, the milk makers.

GOAT

SHEEP

REINDEER

DAIRY COW

Other animals make milk, too. But dairy cows make most of the milk we use.

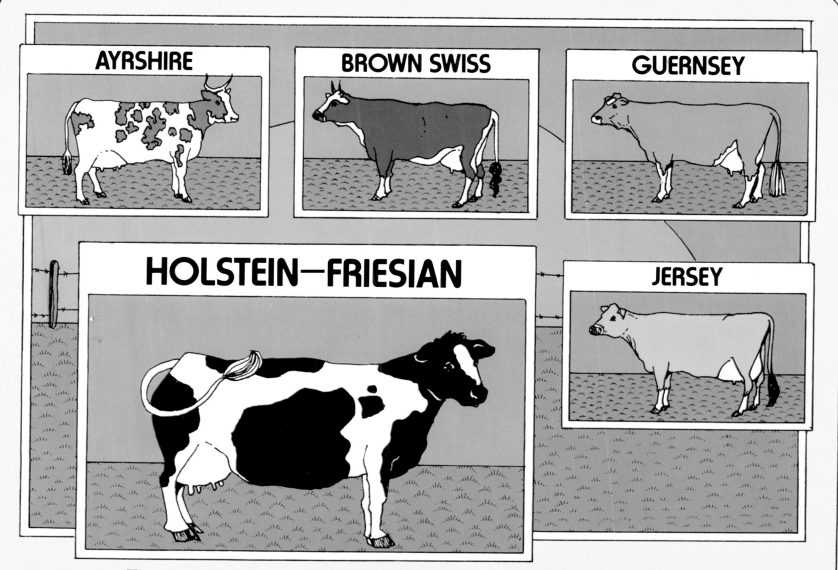

There are five common breeds of dairy cows. The Holstein-Friesian
is the most popular because it can produce more milk
than the other breeds.

A cow is able to make milk when she is two years old and has given birth to a calf. Her milk is the food for her baby. She makes more than her calf will ever need—so we use the extra milk.

A few months after her calf is born, a cow is bred again to have another calf. She will be pregnant for nine months. Two months before her second calf is due, the farmer stops milking her, so she stops producing milk. She is "dry." When her new calf is born, she makes milk again.

In the spring and summer, a dairy cow eats grass and drinks water from streams and ponds. She eats about fifty pounds of food, and drinks about fifteen gallons of water, a day.

During the cold months, a dairy cow is sheltered in a barn.
She is fed hay, winter silage, and grains. The better her food
is, the more milk she will make and the better her milk will be.

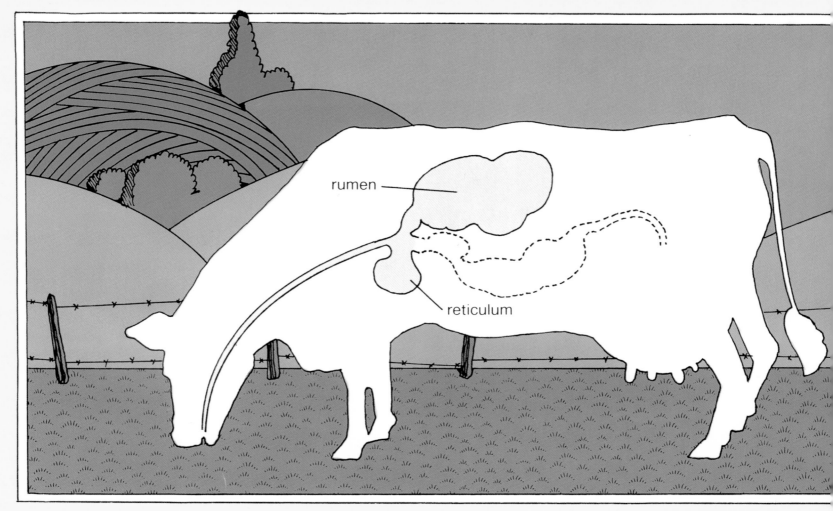

The food eaten by a dairy cow is tough and coarse, and it is hard to digest. So the cow has a special stomach. It has four parts! When the cow eats, she chews just enough to swallow her food. It goes to the first two stomachs, the rumen (roo'min) and the reticulum (ri tik' ya lam). When the cow is full, she rests.

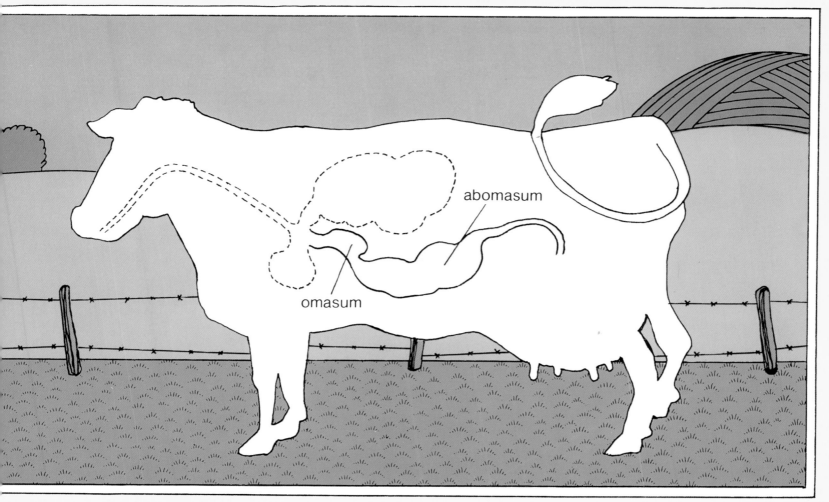

abomasum

omasum

Then, the cow coughs up balls of food called cud. She "chews her cud" thoroughly this time, and then swallows it again. It now goes to the third and fourth stomachs, the omasum (ō mā' sem) and the abomasum (ab' e mā' sem), where it is finally digested.

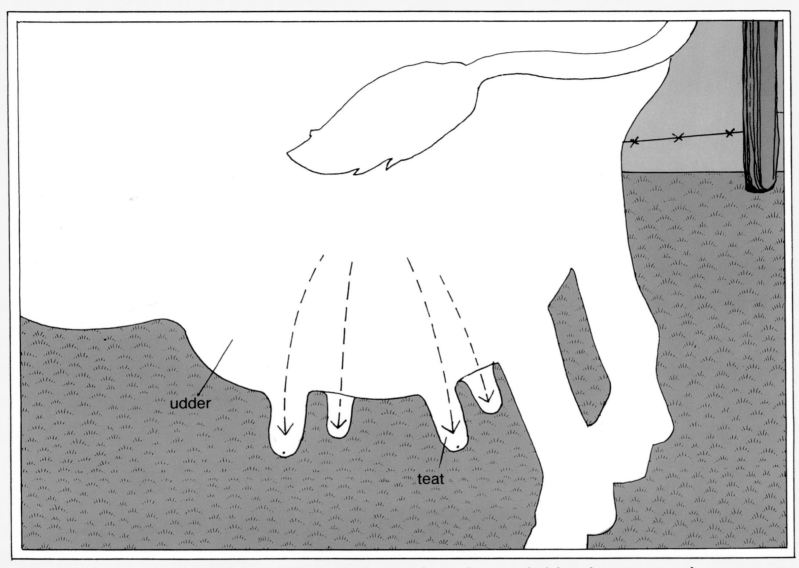

Some of the digested food goes into the cow's bloodstream, and finally enters her udder, where the milk is made. The udder has four nipples, or teats. Milk will come out of her teats.

It is time to milk a dairy cow when her udder is full.
She must be milked once in the morning and once in the
evening. If she isn't milked twice a day, her udder will
become sore and swollen.

A cow can be milked by hand. To do this, the farmer grasps a teat in each of his hands, and squeezes it with thumb and forefinger. Then he gently pulls his hand down the teat. The milk squirts out into a pail.

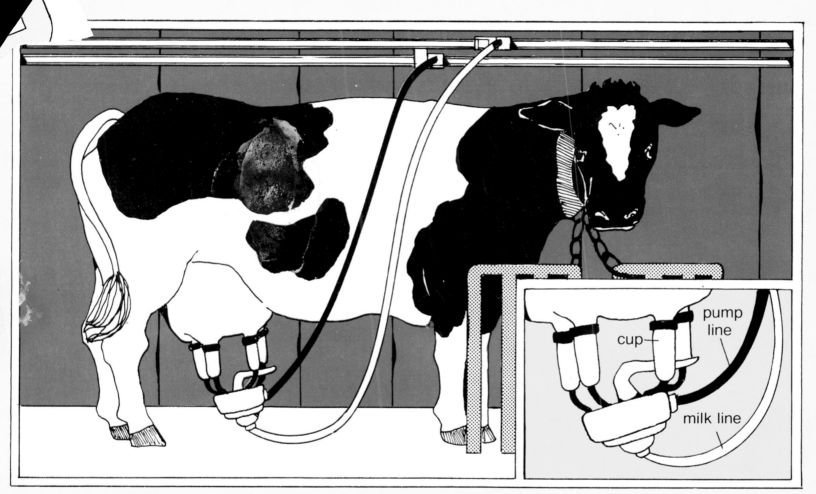

cup

pump
line

milk line

Today most farmers use milking machines, which are quicker and
cleaner. First, the udder must be washed. A small amount of
milk is "stripped" by hand—that is, pulled from the teat to
begin milking. Then a pump sucks the milk through rubber-lined
cups that fit over the cow's teats. The action of the cups is
like the sucking of a calf.

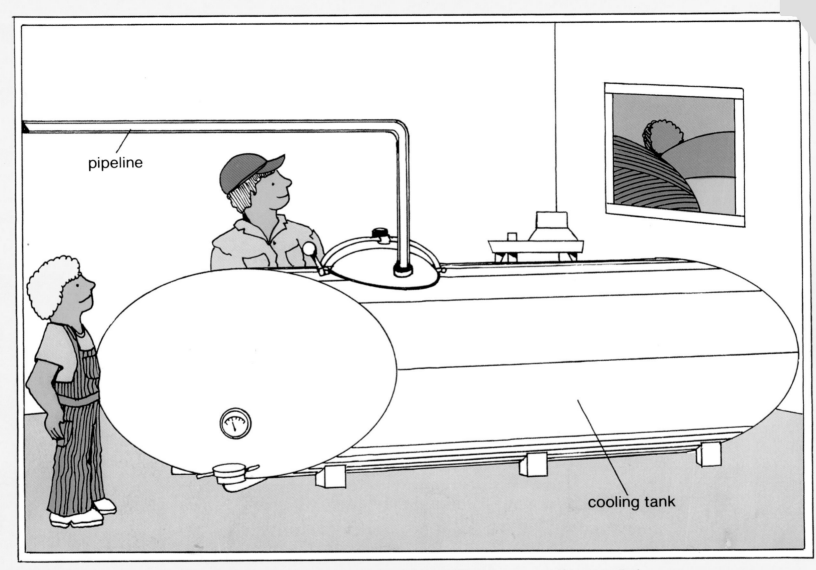

pipeline

cooling tank

The milk then moves through a pipeline to a cooling tank in a separate room. The tank keeps the milk cool—below 40° F. If the milk stayed warm, it might spoil.

Some farmers keep a daily record of how much milk each cow makes.
The average cow makes five gallons a day. Then the farmer
sterilizes and cleans everything he has used, after each milking.

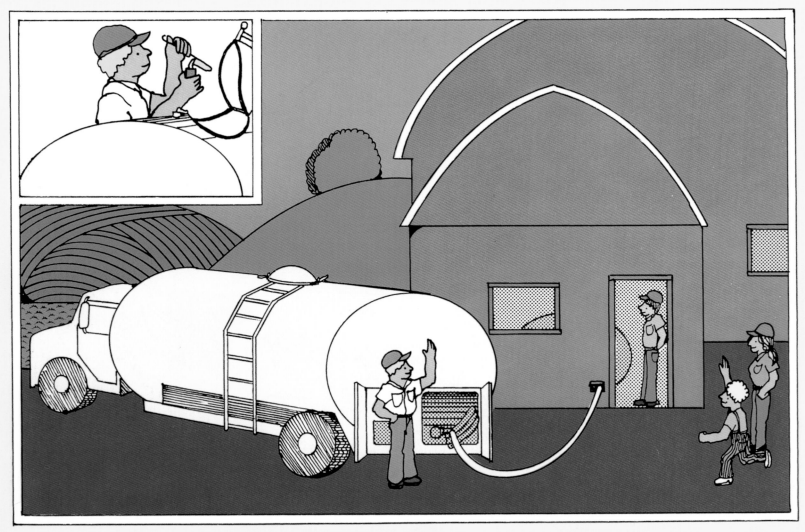

Now the milk is ready to take a trip. Every day, a big, shiny truck comes to the farm. The driver takes a sample of milk to be tested later. Then milk is pumped into the tank of the truck, which is insulated to keep it cool.

The tank truck carries the milk to the dairy.

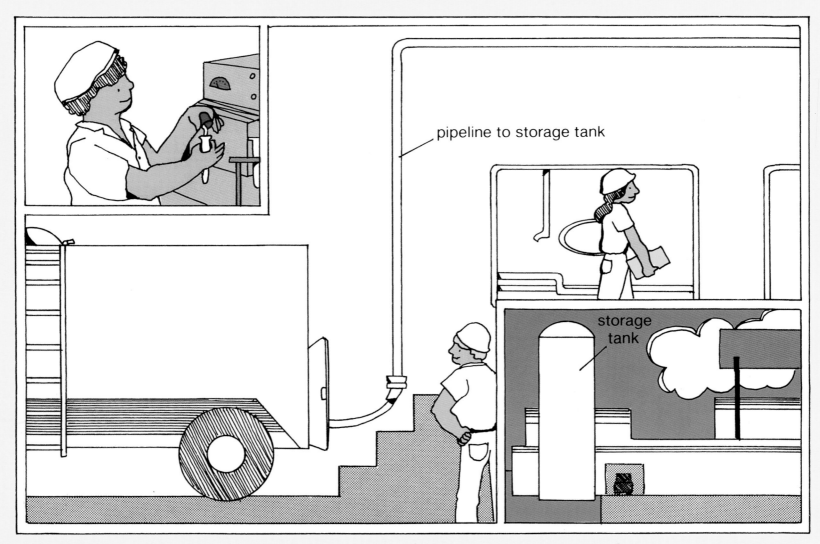

pipeline to storage tank

storage tank

When the truck arrives at the dairy, the workers are ready to begin. The milk sample is tested in a laboratory for butterfat content (butterfat is a part of cream), flavor, odor, and bacteria. Then the milk is pumped into a big refrigerated storage tank.

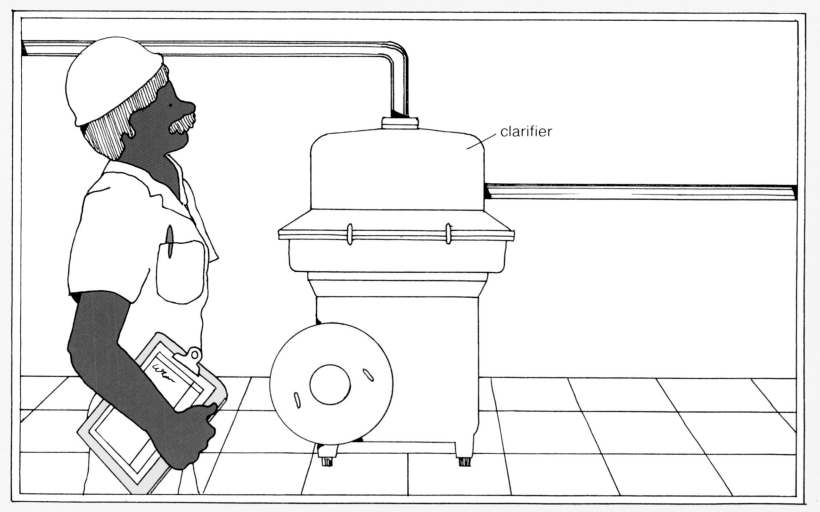

clarifier

Inside the dairy there are many big, noisy machines. The milk is moved from the storage tank into a "clarifier" to be cleaned. The milk in the clarifier has come from many dairy farms, and it doesn't all have the same amount of cream. So it is blended until it is all the same. This is called "standardizing."

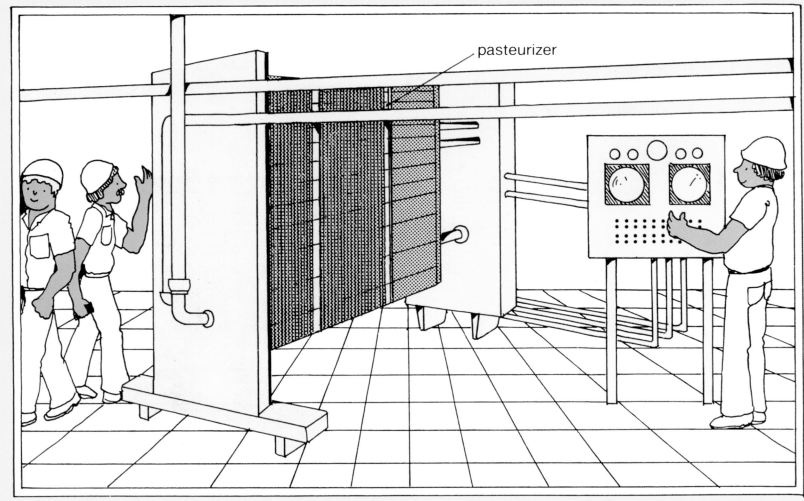

pasteurizer

The milk moves on to be "pasteurized," which means it is heated to kill any disease-causing bacteria. This also helps to make the milk stay fresher, longer. During pasteurization, the milk is heated up to 161° F for at least fifteen seconds and then quickly cooled again.

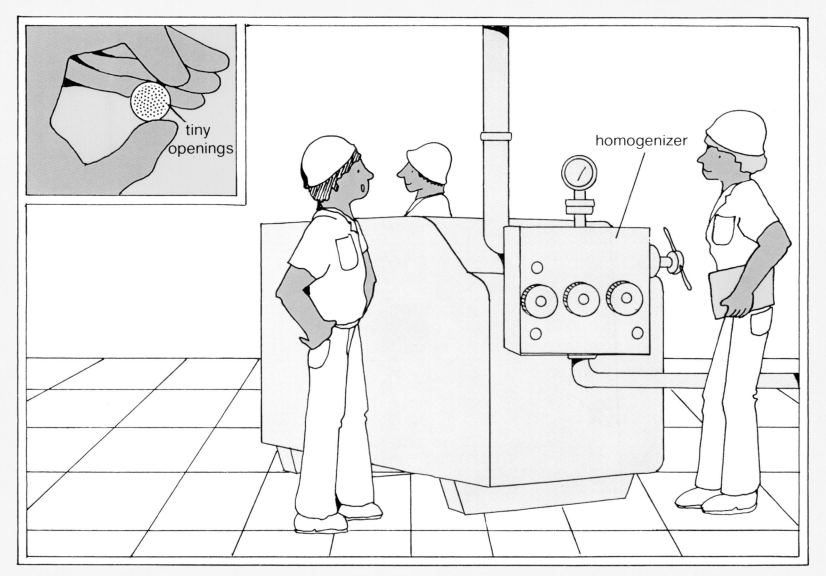

Next, the milk is "homogenized," or forced through tiny openings under great pressure. This breaks up the fatty globules of the cream to give every drop of milk the same amount.

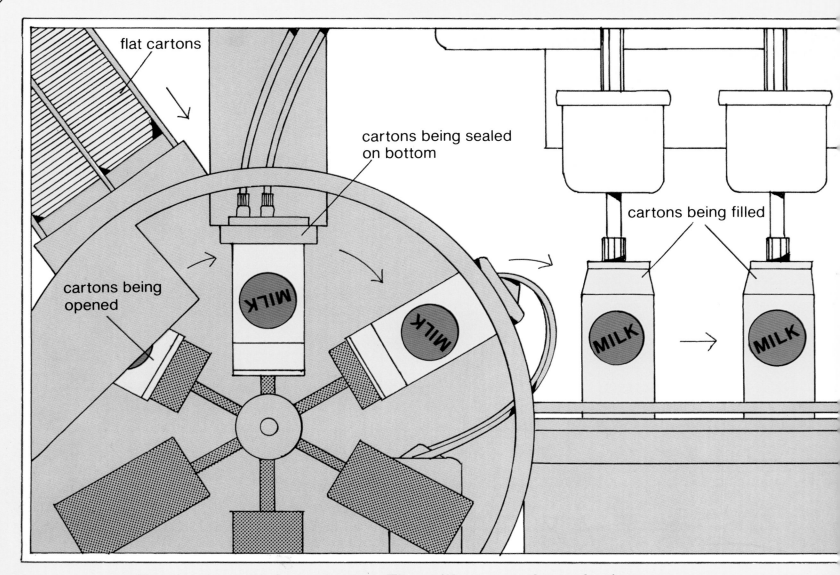

flat cartons

cartons being sealed on bottom

cartons being filled

cartons being opened

MILK

MILK

MILK

MILK

Finally, the milk is packaged. The milk moves through pipes to automatic packaging machines. These machines fill and seal the milk into paper cartons or plastic jugs.

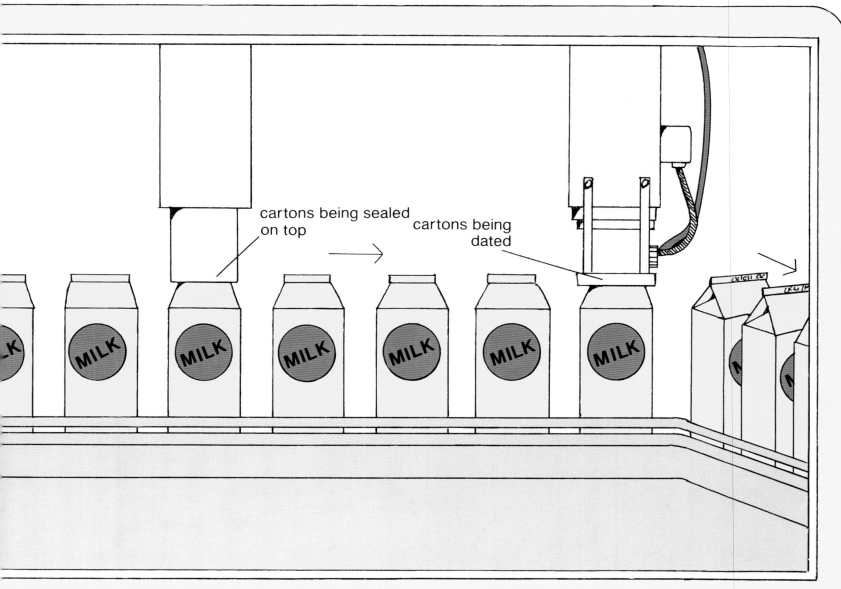

cartons being sealed on top

cartons being dated

Dates are printed on them to show how long the milk will stay fresh.

Then the containers are put into cases and stored in a big refrigerated room. After the dairy workers are through with their work, they clean and sterilize all the equipment.

Delivery trucks come to the dairy, where they are loaded with containers of milk and milk products.

The trucks make deliveries to many stores. The milk is...

placed in coolers, ready for us to buy and enjoy.

Milk and Other Dairy Products

Milk is a nutritious drink that makes our bodies strong and healthy.

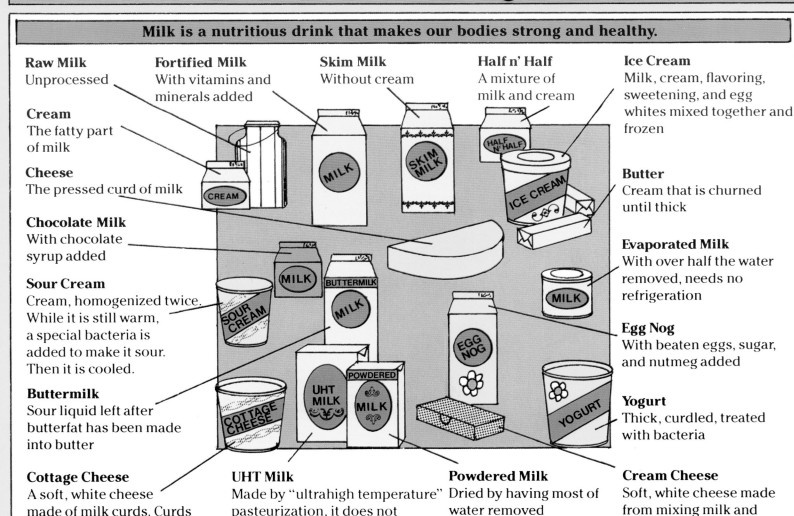

Raw Milk
Unprocessed

Cream
The fatty part
of milk

Cheese
The pressed curd of milk

Chocolate Milk
With chocolate
syrup added

Sour Cream
Cream, homogenized twice.
While it is still warm,
a special bacteria is
added to make it sour.
Then it is cooled.

Buttermilk
Sour liquid left after
butterfat has been made
into butter

Cottage Cheese
A soft, white cheese
made of milk curds. Curds
are a solid that forms
when milk sours.

Fortified Milk
With vitamins and
minerals added

Skim Milk
Without cream

Half n' Half
A mixture of
milk and cream

Ice Cream
Milk, cream, flavoring,
sweetening, and egg
whites mixed together and
frozen

Butter
Cream that is churned
until thick

Evaporated Milk
With over half the water
removed, needs no
refrigeration

Egg Nog
With beaten eggs, sugar,
and nutmeg added

Yogurt
Thick, curdled, treated
with bacteria

UHT Milk
Made by "ultrahigh temperature"
pasteurization, it does not
need refrigeration.

Powdered Milk
Dried by having most of
water removed

Cream Cheese
Soft, white cheese made
from mixing milk and
cream together *or* cream
made into cheese